Garden
of Fairytale Animals

A Curious Collection of
Creatures to Color

Kanoko Egusa

There is a mysterious key that appears once every few years,

an important key needed to open a door to a peculiar place.

This secret door is deep in the woods,

so the animals take their time carrying

the key through the forest,

enjoying everything the seasons have to offer on the way.

They marvel at kittens playing in a pleasant spring garden,

hydrangeas and summer grass floating along the water,

raccoons celebrating the autumn harvest,

and the magical light illuminating a winter church.

Beautiful colors breathe life into the seasonal foliage,

and the animals slowly wander closer to the door.

Upon reaching the door and sliding in the key . . .

It opens to welcome them to the mystical

Garden of Fairytale Animals.

About the Author

Kanoko Egusa |ILLUSTRATOR, ARTIST

Kanoko Egusa was born in Sendai, Japan. After graduating from university, she studied professional design and drawing at a vocational school in Kanazawa and started to work as a freelance graphic designer in 2008. In 2011, she began kanoko egusa design atelier, creating illustrations depicting imaginary worlds filled with animals, flowers, and plants.

In her studio, Kanoko surrounds herself with the things and images that inspire her. She takes inspiration from nature and from antique books, postcards, and greeting cards. One of her favorite artists is John Tenniel, and she's studied the style and technique of his illustrations for *Alice's Adventures in Wonderland*. As a child she enjoyed the *Tom and Jerry* show, Disney films, Beatrix Potter's *The Tale of Peter Rabbit*, and Tasha Tudor's illustrated children's books.

Kanoko begins each piece of art simply, hand drawing using a dip pen and ink. She then digitizes each illustration to make any adjustments and finishing touches. With each illustration, she seeks to capture vivid expressions and magical moments, full of emotion and life.

Look for Kanoko's other fully illustrated coloring book

Kingdom of Curious Creatures

Escape to a magical place where French Bulldogs mind the farmer's market vegetable stand, piglets nap in teacups, critters play chess, and hares throw a wedding to remember. In this charming coloring book for adults, you'll find colored examples to inspire you and new and enchanting fairytale art that you've never seen before. Bring imaginative scenes to life using your favorite coloring tools and express your creativity!

Garden
of
Fairytale
Animals

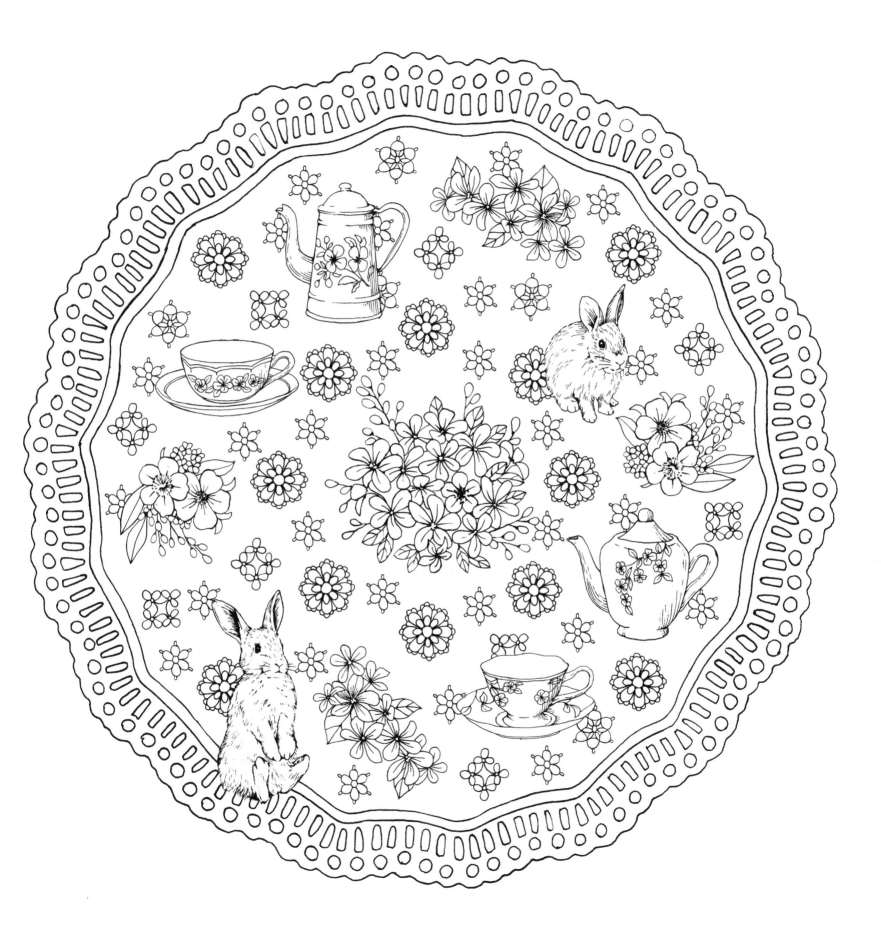

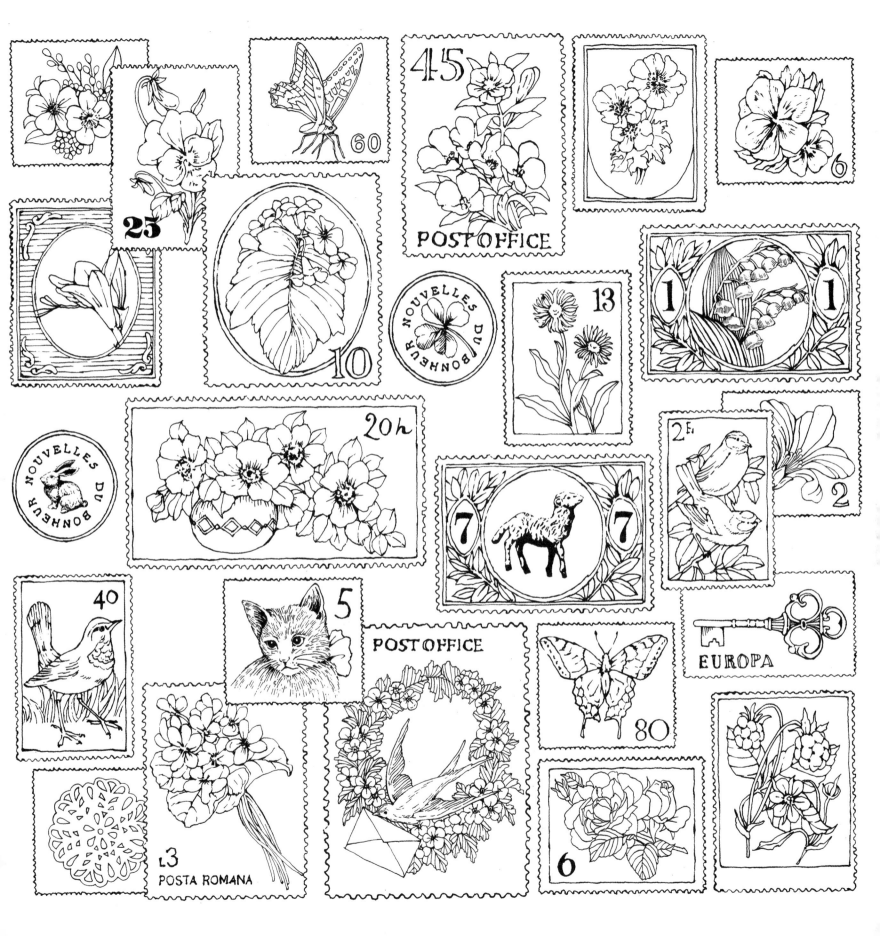

Garden of Fairytale Animals is a revised translation of the original Japanese book MORI GA KANADERU RHAPSODY=*Rhapsody in the forest*.
This version published by New Design Originals Corporation, an imprint of Fox Chapel Publishing Company, Inc., Mount Joy, PA.

All colored samples were prepared by the publisher, not from guidance supplied by the author herself.

ISBN 978-1-4972-0571-0

Fox Chapel focuses on providing real value to our customers through the printing and book production process.
We strive to select quality paper that is also eco-friendly. This book is printed on archival-quality, acid-free paper that can be expected
to last for at least 200 years. It meets the minimum requirements of the American National Standard for Information Sciences—Permanence of
Paper for Printed Library Materials, ANSI/NISO Z39.48-1992. This book is printed on paper produced from trees harvested from
well-managed forests where measures are taken to protect wildlife, plants, and water quality.

We are always looking for talented authors. To submit an idea, please send a brief inquiry to acquisitions@foxchapelpublishing.com.

Printed in China
Fourth printing